MAGIC CITY GOSPEL

MAGIC CITY GOSPEL

POEMS

ASHLEY M. JONES

HUB CITY PRESS
SPARTANBURG, SC

First printing, January 2017
Book design: Meg Reid

Cover Art © A'Driane Nieves

TEXT Adobe Garamond 10.5 / 15
DISPLAY TT Chocolates 15/13.4

Library of Congress Cataloging-in-
Publication Data

Names: Jones, Ashley M., 1990- author.
Title: Magic City Gospel : poems / Ashley M. Jones.
Description: Spartanburg SC : Hub City Press, 2017.
Includes bibliographical references.
Identifiers: LCCN 2016029313 | ISBN 9781938235269
Classification: LCC PS3610.O595 A6 2017 | DDC
811/.6—dc23
LC record available at https://lccn.loc.
gov/2016029313

HUB CITY
PRESS

186 West Main St.
Spartanburg, SC 29306
1.864.577.9349

for Donald, Jennifer, Monique, Jasmine, and Julian

for Birmingham

TABLE OF CONTENTS

Sam Cooke Sings to Me when I Am Afraid   3
(I'm Blue) The Gong Gong Song, or, America the Beautiful   4
Eating Red Dirt in Greensboro, Alabama   5
nem   6
Addie, Carole, Cynthia, Denise   7
Teaching J To read   8
Sammy Davis Jr. Sings to Mike Brown, Jr.   9
Rammer Jammer   10
Sonnet for Sopping   12
Mock Election   13
Prayer   14
In The Beginning, There Was A Sound   15
The men come for Emmett and Tamir and Michael and Eric
and John and Trayvon and...   16
De Soto, Discoverer   18
De Soto Leaves a Negro   19
God Speaks to Alabama   20
Salat Behind Al's Mediterranean and American Food   21
Birmingham Fire and Rescue   22
Robert Chambliss Lays the Bombs   23
The first time I heard about slavery   24
Viewing a KKK Uniform at the Civil Rights Institute   25
What the Glass Eye Saw   26
slaves for sale   27
Elegy   28
How To Make Your Daughters Culturally Aware and Racially
Content During Christmastime   30
Poem for Revolution   32

What It Means To Say Sally Hemings   33

spin•ster   34

Alabama Recipe Box: Cornbread, 1862   35

List of Famous Alabama Slaves   36

Ingredient list: black girl   37

The Ballad of Pearl Bailey   38

Corn Silk Barbie   39

Gregory Hines comes in a Vision   40

Birmingham Fire and Rescue Haiku, 1963   41

Symphony of God—A Hymn to Our Jesus   42

The History Books Have Forgotten Horace King   44

On Martin Luther King Day, A Noose Is Hung On A Tree
In Blount County   46

Virgin Mary, Re-Imagined   47

Happiness   48

Gospel of the Grits   49

Coming of Age   50

Sojurner Truth Speaks to Her Daughter, 1843   52

Riddled In the Heart of Dixie   53

ACKNOWLEDGEMENTS   57

NOTES   59

Sam Cooke plays on the cassette deck in our Nissan Sentra. I am strapped like a parachuter in my booster seat. It is Saturday night. We are travelling from grandma's house in Bessemer, having waited until the night's third episode of "Walker, Texas Ranger" to leave for home. I am scared because I am not touching my mother. Sam Cooke is crooning about a party or a lost love or a change coming, and I'm afraid to die. Tonight, Alabama doesn't feel like home—it is too dark to see and the alleys beckon our little car to them. Dad knows all the shortcuts because he's a fireman, and I wish so hard for the interstate with lights and its fast, homeward promise. I wish for our little home and all my toys, even the ones that scare me at night. I wish for morning, when I will eat collard greens and cornbread with Mom. I wish for playtime with Monique and our blue couch that is a jungle, that is Pride Rock, that is a spaceship. Sam Cooke is painfully singing. He's screaming. I can barely breathe behind all these straps—I am straightjacketed and trying to understand the hurt in Sam Cooke's voice, and why does grandma never get up from her easy chair? Why does she look out at us like we are this night—like we are something she will never quite touch? Even when she laughs, why does she still look sad? Why have we not made it home yet? If I close my eyes and reach for sleep, can I make us teleport home? Sam Cooke, give me the answers instead of your steely wail.

(I'M BLUE) THE GONG GONG SONG, OR, AMERICA THE BEAUTIFUL

Ike Turner sailed the ocean blue in nineteen hundred sixty-two.

Brown baby boy with a guitar for a ship—the treble clef shining black as a sail. Ike, make like a sailor and break the waves of water, waves of sound.

On the horizon, amber waves of Anna Mae. The plump promise of fruit in her dark Tennessee body. Nutbush woman, wild with the blues, Ike dreams of you feverishly. That big, wailing mouth. Those legs—shotguns waiting to be loaded up with bullet beats. Ike imagines the way they would feel in his hands, the click of a calf, the smooth, ample ankle. Anna Mae is much softer than she looks from far away. Easier to press a thumb, a fist, into.

What good is an explorer if he doesn't keep his discoveries down? Ike Turner gave you a name, America. It alliterated and it sold them records, baby. Tina Turner, baby. He *found* you, baby. He made you *live*.

When he speaks, you will listen:

"I brought you in this world and I can take you out. Bit by glistening bit. You would have gotten hit with something, anyway—smallpox would have made it over the ocean without me. I built your immunity, baby. Thank me for your scars. Doesn't matter what you call me, I made you sing. From my mouth comes gold.

Tell me you can hear a jukebox playing 'Proud Mary' without something buckling in your highbrow hips. Tell me something doesn't stir you to gyrate to 'The Gong Gong Song.' I'm ringing your bell. I'm making you dance. You ain't got to love me, baby, but you better know who I am.

I'm Red, White, and Blue. Shoo Bay Do Bay Do Bay Do."

EATING RED DIRT IN GREENSBORO, ALABAMA

I ate red dirt for the first time
with Aunt Hattie—big, brown blind angel
who listened to local crimes

on her police scanner. Its monotone lullaby
crooned all through the night, piercing, faithful.
When she heard it was my first time,

she sent us to the hill. We scraped it off, tried
to ignore the ants and the strange, dull
sour scent. Stealing dirt, a local crime,

only punished by whatever was hiding inside
our Ziploc bags: a pillbug, a ladybug's broken shell.
Back from the hunt, for the first time

I realized how citified
I really was, scared of something so full
of local germs. But was it a crime

to fear eating dirt? Finally, my Southern pride
made me put it to my lips, resist the acidic pull
of bile in my throat. And for the first time,
I felt like a local, swallowing this bittersweet crime.

NEM

pronoun \nem\

1. and them, especially in the American South

A.

You finally get the courage to use the word when you're sixteen. When you finally wear a real bra and can count on your hips to fit into a skirt the right way. Your tongue is a bit looser these days— you even get the jokes when you're talking with your mom and all the women in her family. When grandmother squeals out a dig at someone you don't know, you find something slippery in it and laugh, finally, with the throat of a woman. Someone asks you who you went to the store with the other day. *Mama'nem*, you say. Inside, you tilt with excitement. You light up, a pinball machine of colloquialisms.

B.

At school, you've become a comedian. You're quick with jokes about race—you're the only black girl in most of your classes. It is easy to blend in and stand out. You offer opinions when they are required—during Black History Month, during the unit on the Atlantic Slave Trade, when you and the teacher are the only ones who can name a black poet who is not Langston Hughes. You have perfected what you call "the Klansman:" a short impression you pull out when there's no more conversation amongst your peers. They are impressed with your feigned Southern accent. They are more impressed with how you wield the n-word. *Me, Billy-Ray'annem gon' round up some niggers*, you say. You watch your classmates laugh. Their eyes bulge like hot dough.

ADDIE, CAROLE, CYNTHIA, DENISE

Amen, Alabama.
Bring in the Dixie sun,
      cover us in the
delicate, glassy sunshine
      erupting all over.
Find us, fevered, in the
      glen, Jones Valley.
Have you seen the churches with windows stained?
      Infinite steeples,
just turn any corner. Do you
      know how we bleed, like Jesus?
Loud vibrato
      melting the Sunday sky,
new mercies exploding, dynamite,
      over our brown bodies.
Pretty little ones, dressed in lace, beneath
      quivering old ones in hose and hats.
Remember how 16th Street shook,
      symphony of fiery coughs
that turned our Birmingham to blood.
      Under what God's hand did we die like this?

Villains, victors, what did *you* see?
      Wa wa watermelon, a chorus of coons,
X's on the eyes, a grim cartoon?
      Y'all come back now, hear?
Zippety do dah till the day you die.

TEACHING J TO READ

I don't know how to begin,
how to explain that *A* means *A*,
that *B* isn't *Beaver*
but simply *B*,
the second drawing
in a series of twenty-six.

He is in the fifth grade
and he can't read about Dick or Jane.
He spends his days
finding new places to hide—
in between book chapters, scraping ink;
at the end of a punchline;
on the lip of a carton of milk.

I am useless, like an after-school special—
here, there is no purple dinosaur,
no sparkle in our smiles,
no bell-toned music to montage this away.

He finds *pig* in *big*
and the way a fist can solve these things.

He loses his name
in the sprawling alphabet—
the surest letter is the first: *J.*
This is the dark curve
that marks him,
and, even now,
I can't remember the letters
that follow.

SAMMY DAVIS JR. SINGS TO MIKE BROWN JR.

You're clear out of this world, Michael. You're a blueblack star.
I'm ringing with the sound of your spit on the pavement,
the shine of your blood. I look into your wet, gulping eyes
and see my glass eye reflected, flatly in your pupils.
I pour a whole note into each bullet hole.
I string my song through you—
straight seam to keep you for the next world.
One chord of kisses for each of your upturned hands, Michael.
One note per finger, the *tsk tsk* of your palms, cymbals holding sound.
When my song is done, I will wait for you to sing,
for the flaming *o* of your mouth to soften
and spread—are you baritone, bass? Do you sing
in a wail with ricocheting vibrato, or is your song
a ringing plea in 4/4 time?

RAMMER JAMMER

George Wallace Stands in the Schoolhouse Door, June 11, 1963

Between the thighs
of the doorway,
you are powerful.
The confetti of camera clicks
and your smart business suit
and the swamp of teenaged protesters
swaddle you with sweat.
Important men
from Washington have come
to clear you out.
Tension,
thick and bitter
as a watermelon rind.
From the doorway,
you see Vivian and James
waiting in the government car.
They wish to register here.
From the doorway,
you see walls and waves of
ballot-faced whites.
They are checkmarks
in the next election.
It is only after
your speech is delivered
that you realize how thirsty you are—
your cottonmouth
is unbecoming
for a state leader.

How nice it would be
to sit on your porch
with Lurleen and a glass of sweet tea.
How nice it would be
to get out of this heat
and out of Tuscaloosa
and back to marbled Montgomery
and its halls that echo—
obedient, loud, and white.

SONNET FOR SOPPING

My mother ate with hands instead of forks,
a cone of fingers, collard greens contorted
into a dripping package, seasoning
the cornbread tucked inside—pinto beans
sitting on top. What special flavors hide
inside thumb, index, middle, ring, what slides
through that is lost on the cold teeth of a fork?
Something in a hand says *salt, garlic, pork.*
It is cast iron, it tastes better with age—
the skin a bouillion, a succulent cage
carried from Africa, to slaves, farmers,
maids and sharecroppers. When did we embrace
the colonial cuffs of silverware
so that even our food assimilates?

We spent all of high school making fun of George W. Bush and his satellite ears and his little-eyed smile and the way he heaved at his own tiny jokes. We hated him for Iraq and Afghanistan and Iran and the Axis of Evil and for the strange way he loved Condoleezza. We hated him because he was not Bill Clinton, who we only knew because he ate McDonald's, and because impeach sounded golden, like an ice cream flavor. We blamed him, as we debated during lunch and at P.E., for our guilt when we stared at the Middle Eastern kids. We denounced him when we said how brave it was for our Muslim friends to sneak away to the empty gymnasium, their prayer mats angled to the East. We threw up our first two fingers like hippies, and we felt sad for the kids whose parents had that "W" bumper sticker. We voted for anyone but him in the mock election. We brandished the soft weapons of our vocabularies— incompetent, recount, deficit. We called ourselves patriotic as we chattered down the hallways, and we wore "I voted" stickers on our chests like lieutenants.

PRAYER

Our Father who art in Heaven,
let me tell you how it is:
the cool girls at school
make fun of my lunch every day,
and you, Father, are uniquely qualified
to end my woes.

Father,
please tell mama to buy the daintier deli meats—
black forest ham, honey roasted turkey—
instead of fat, cold bologna.

Guide her unchanging hand toward honey mustard
and those pretty little pickles cut into discs.
Let her find peace in whole wheat bread.

Guide her, Father,
past those big, delicious chocolate muffins
that they say look moldy.
I'm tired of stowing them away
in the bottom of my backpack.

Or, even better, Father,
and only if you have the time,
could you open her tight-lipped purse
and let lunch money flow from it into my hands
so I can slide a plastic tray down the buffet
and groan on meatloaf Monday?

Heavenly Father,
deliver me from lunchtime hell,
in Your son's name—
he was a kid once, surely—amen.

IN THE BEGINNING, THERE WAS A SOUND

After I was born,
I cried for three months straight.
My mouth, a great brown crack
in the Alabama soil,
sprouted wondrous wails.
My tongue,
a cotton candy spade,
licked the air,
and it tasted of ticking
and the salt
of baby formula.
Each day,
I was a siren.
Five o' clock, exactly,
and I'd scream until nightfall.
Alive, I said.
Pain, I said.
Maybe I stopped
because it is hard
to keep roaring.
Maybe because
I felt the warm burn
of my mother's
loving ear.
Maybe,
because I grew hoarse,
and at some point,
there's nothing
more to do
with a voice
than to hum drum
and whisper
as loud
as you can.

THE MEN COME FOR EMMETT AND TAMIR AND MICHAEL AND ERIC AND JOHN AND TRAYVON AND...

after Gwendolyn Brooks

Tonight, he dreams of sunshine, the blood
browned in a pan of grandma's neckbones,
field flowers and the quiet
river, the stars and their nighttime school.

Tonight is dark and still and mild,
the air unfazed by the pursuit
Emmett hears before he sees.

Brown prince, whistling that whistle
that hadn't meant anything,
but set men's pulses beating fast.

What is a black boy but a villain?
His black eyes. The way he goes about
his black business. His towering
black height. His slang-cluttered speech.

Tamir Rice was a man, the police write,
larger than a child, a wolf. What softness,
after all, is there in a villain?

What was four and a half hours in the sun
to Michael who never guessed he would die
from the metallic tantrums
of an officer's gun? Maybe there was something
in the air that whispered open season.

In Staten Island, they laid into Eric.
They laid their hands on him like hurried pastors.
And, his body laid heavy on his wife

in her dreams, in her pocketbook, in her children, though
it was too late to do anything about it,
to hear those last three words.
Did John have time to raise his hands
in the aisles of plastic darts and BB guns?
Is a black boy not loved by his black mother?
Does his soul glitter with something startling and black?

DE SOTO, DISCOVERER

"Never before had our soil been trodden by European feet! Never before had our natives beheld white faces, long beards, strange apparel, glittering armor, and, stranger than all, the singular animals bestrode by the dashing cavaliers! De Soto had discovered Alabama, not by sea, but after dangerous and difficult marches had penetrated her northeastern border with a splendid and well equipped land expedition."

—History of Alabama, and Incidentally of Georgia and Mississippi, Albert James Pickett

We are dashing—
Cary Grant conquistador,
Clark Gable on horseback,
halitosis blazing on our tongues.

Cuba was a chest of gems
but gold is laced in Alabama's teeth—
at least, that's what they told us,
and what is a word but a map?

Now, the natives.
We know them with arrows
and some with God
in their throats,
but our reply is metallic
and unbending.
You bow or you die.

They are just specks
of dark soil in our path.
We will wash up with seawater
and make them puddle,
native mud.

Even the blistering sunset
knows our names—
it whispers
as it curtsies, equatorially—
España, manifesto,
this world is yours.

DE SOTO LEAVES A NEGRO

"After twenty-five days had been passed at the capital of Coosa, De Soto marched in the direction of the Tallapoosa, leaving behind a Christian negro, too sick to travel, whom the Indians desired to retain among them on account of his singular hair and sable complexion. He recovered, and was doubtless the distant ancestor of the dark-colored savages seen in that region in more modern times."

—*History of Alabama, and Incidentally of Georgia and Mississippi,* Albert James Pickett

A gift of sick skin.
A sac of black and bronze.
You are presented
alongside two swine,
a few discs of bacon
and fatback—
a body is a body is a body.

The armada strode like God
across the water—
America, a jungle promising gold.
You will leave this cavalry
at Tallapoosa.
You will watch them march
with destiny in their heels,
and you will heal
among these brown people.

Years from now,
your sons will walk, darkly,
along these banks,
their skin beating
with the sickness
of the chain and the whip.

They will look upon
their beating skin
and hear you singing—
their eyes will swirl
with pride, riverside.

GOD SPEAKS TO ALABAMA

I molded you
from red clay, sweet cornbread,
the slow drip of a lemon
squeezed over sugar and ice.
I kissed you to life, on the lips.
Mama bird I am—
my tongue feeds you blood.
I have waited
in this heat for you
to pucker
and say my name—
Hallelujah, Alabama.
I give you fire
and blackberries
and white, thick cotton.
I give you the honeybee
and the yellowhammer—
find me, swallow me down
and whisper me
to passersby
as you sit, nightly,
on the creaky
front porch.

SALAT BEHIND AL'S MEDITERRANEAN AND AMERICAN FOOD

This evening, in Birmingham,
when I'm meeting a friend
for fried chicken
and poetry,
you prostrate before God
on a piece of cardboard box
in the back alley.
Beside you, there is a dumpster
whispering styrofoam
and onion skins.
The shells of dead cockroaches
bend and crackle
under your knees. Even they pray.
The backdoor of the restaurant
and the towering
University Parking Deck
shelter you in shadow.
Fifteen minutes from now,
you will bring me cheap fries
and fingers,
and when you ask me
if I'd like ketchup,
your accent heavy as oil,
it sounds like a proverb—
clean tomato,
sovereign God.

BIRMINGHAM FIRE AND RESCUE

Our father was a beacon
of fire and water—
we drove the family van
to Station 29
and he washed it there
while we played in the concrete yard.
Back then, he was not
assistant chief
or paramedic,
and we were not too old
to give him kisses
at his command.
There was something
about that water—
fireman's water—
that charmed us, spooked us,
gave us pause to its mystery.
It could eat fire alive.
But, when he was rinsing the van,
it was a plaything—
it broke, somehow, into little clear gems
for us to run through—
a shower of mist and light
to cool us
in the Alabama heat.

ROBERT CHAMBLISS LAYS THE BOMBS

How softly
he carried them,
how quietly
they slept
in the back
of his little house.

They are toothy
and sticky
with heat.

Tonight,
he must leave them,
lonely
and unwatched.
He says a prayer
as he departs.
As he sleeps,
he will think of them.

THE FIRST TIME I HEARD ABOUT SLAVERY

was in 1993, sitting on our scratchy yellow couch watching "Roots," sandwiched between Mom and Dad. "Roots" is a Black family tradition—come February, come Kunta Kinte and his wild eyes. Come the inhuman wail and the severing of Kunta's runaway ankle-bone. That first night, I was three years old. My eyes were too small to swallow that far-off, bright country where Kunta lived. Too small to open around the whole sea and its ships that sailed and sailed. No one explained that I would not become a slave, too, that my skin was not a modern-day marker of things to come. My fingers had never bled, so I did not understand the pain of picking cotton. I did not understand the meaning of light skin and the after-dark work of house slaves. I did not understand the curse of soft breasts peeking, brightly, through a cotton dress. I only knew the couch and the TV and my parents who didn't seem to fear the whips. That night, I felt alone in my bedroom. I could barely hear my older sister breathing in the bunk above me, and that darkness meant that tomorrow, it might all come true. So I didn't sleep. I keep my small eyes wide and guarded the life I had come to know.

VIEWING A KKK UNIFORM AT THE CIVIL RIGHTS INSTITUTE

All you can really tell at first
is that it was starched.
Some Betty Sue, Marge, Jane,
some proper girl
with a great black iron
made those corners sharp.
The hood, white and ablaze
with creases,
body flat and open
for husband, brother, son.
Behind the glass,
it seems frozen, waiting
for summer night
to melt it into action,
for the clean white flame
of God to awaken its limbs.
In front of it, you are dwarfed—
you imagine a pair of pupils
behind the empty holes
of the mask.
Behind the stiff cotton,
would the eyes squint
to see through small white slits,
or would they open wide
as a burning house
to hunt you down
until you pooled
like old rope
before them?

WHAT THE GLASS EYE SAW

for Sammy Davis, Jr.

Back doors, wood floors.
Whites only on little square signs
all around the hotel.
The scuffs taps leave on stages.
The twinkle in Old Blue's Eye.
Rubies and diamonds on ten nimble fingers.
Black tuxedo jackets,
white cigarettes,
chandeliers glowing and cold champagne,
towers of pomade jars
and scented oils
and black shoe polish.
Ten pretty dancers in frills and feathers,
the little sassy one whose back fits easily
in an open palm.
A room full of tables
draped in white cloths.
The waiter serving sherry
and the piano player's thick brown hands.
The mirrored, metallic, blackskinned
shoes for tonight's all new revue.
The black backsides
of the world's smiling white teeth.

SLAVES FOR SALE

"In the land of the Ibo, the Hausa, and the Yoruba, what is the price per barrel of nigrescence?"—Harryette Mullen, "Denigration"

come all come one come all. this one's twenty this one's young this one's got curls for days days days mornings curls eggs and toast curls toast and jam curls pretty little pancake breasts curls afternoons curls nights curls curls and they're everywhere.

shuffle hop step shuffle hop step

one is tall one is strong how many are black black blue black? i'll give you three dark for one light. this one talks jungle talk ooh oohs and aaah aahs. monkey talk. banana talk. blues talk. grasshopper jumpin' jive. shuck jive jive turkey.

flap hop step flap hop step

and now for the kiddies: bill tim bill tim tom tom tim. a buck a piece. a buck a piece. a buck. a buck. strong buck black buck. get em while they're hot sirs get em hot sirs they're hot. buy one none free.

shuck jive shuck jive and it don't stop

ELEGY

for Amiri Baraka

Is it better to die
a LeRoi
or the full Baraka,
screaming bloody verse
with your last black breath?
How many more beats
were in you
on that surgery table,
and will your heaven
be powerful
and Black?

Yours is a graph
we'll trace in stanzas.
The upward trend—
power, metaphor,
America arranged
in shades of brown.
The scattered points
left out of the line—
flame, discomfort,
a potluck of politics.

You were not our flower,
Baraka,
but our fertilizer—
our fish guts,
cow manure,

fierce-smelling
medicine
made for proper growth.

I take you under my tongue
and you are bitter,
an aspirin chewed without water,
a pot of beige rutabagas
without that dash of sugar.
But I will take you again
and again,
even if, sometimes,
I chase you with something sweeter—
a raisin from Langston,
Zora's afternoon teacake.

HOW TO MAKE YOUR DAUGHTERS CULTURALLY AWARE AND RACIALLY CONTENT DURING CHRISTMASTIME

Remind them:
Jesus is Black.
Despite the pictures Granny
has hung on the wall,
despite the glowing good old boy
on her pile of church fans,
Jesus was a brother.
A bruh, not a bro.
Hair of wool, you tell them.

Buy a new nativity set.
Mary with her press and curl,
Joseph with a fade,
baby Jesus fresh out the womb
and curly.

Go to a roadside Christmas shop.
Buy a pale, smiling Santa.
Let your daughters wonder
how he turned brown overnight—
how Santa's face became just like their own,
brown and buttery, a Yuletide miracle.

When you're trimming your plastic tree—
the one you've had since the 80's,
put on "Rudolph" bopped by the Temptations,
"Deck the Halls" by Smokey,
Donny Hathaway's "This Christmas,"
and Gladys Knight's deep, brown voice crooning "Jingle Bells."

Fill the tree skirt
with tightly-wrapped gifts.
Anticipate
your daughters' unbreakable smiles

when they rip off the paper
to reveal an army

of Black Barbies
and brown baby dolls.

POEM FOR REVOLUTION

for Malcolm, Martin and all the rest

the boys and the girls are black.
the dolls and the trucks are black.

the momma and the daddy are black.
the road and the sky are black.

the Bibles and the bullets are black.
the Father and the Son are black.

the water and the fountain are black.
the fire and hoses are black.

the shoes are black. the mouths are black.
the singers and the songs, black.

the caskets and the weepers are black.

the chaff and the wheat are black.
the wind rolls, blackly, through the fields.

WHAT IT MEANS TO SAY SALLY HEMINGS

Bright Girl Sally
Mulatto Sally
Well Dressed Sally
Sally With the Pretty Hair
Sally With the Irish Cotton Dress
Sally With the Smallpox Vaccine
Sally, Smelling of Clean White Soap
Sally Never Farmed A Day In Her Life
Available Sally
Nursemaid Sally
Sally, Filled with Milk
Sally Gone to Paris with Master's Daughter
Sally in the Chamber with the President
Sally in the Chamber with the President's Brother
Illiterate Sally
Capable Sally
Unmarried Sally
Sally, Mother of Madison, Harriet, Beverly, Eston
Sally, Mother of Eston Who Changed His Name
Sally, Mother of Eston Hemings Jefferson
Eston, Who Made Cabinets
Eston, Who Made Music
Eston, Who Moved to Wisconsin
Eston, Whose Children Were Jeffersons
Eston, Who Died A White Man
Grandmother Sally of the White Hemingses
Infamous Sally
Silent Sally
Sally, Kept at Monticello Until Jefferson's Death
Sally, Whose Children Were Freed Without Her

SPIN·STER

spin•ster
noun \\'spin(t)-stər\

1. a woman whose occupation is to spin

I am caught in a revolving door. This is unlike the princess at the wheel, waiting for Rumpelstilskin's tinny laugh and pecking eyes. The days just keep seeping out of the calendar's mouth like phlegm. I have not felt the bristle of moustache hair in years. I would spin it into the finest cloth.

2. *archaic* : an unmarried woman of gentle family

My mother got married when she was twenty-seven. She met my father in college—that's how it's done. That's when nice young boys and nice young girls converge. In Alabama, the least you can do is meet a nice co-ed when you're swimming knee-deep in them. In Alabama, marriage is the next step—high school, college, marriage. Then career. If career. Then kids. Always kids.

3. a woman who seems unlikely to marry

When I was ten, I chose the boy with the unibrow who wore a pleather jacket in the springtime. I didn't wear lip gloss because it felt like VapoRub. I didn't wear skirts because my legs were too skinny. He walked with me, let his arm touch mine, let his eyebrow ripple with intrigue when I walked his way. This was it.

But no boy likes to be put in a corner. No boy likes to be owned.

He said he hated me and took another girl to the dance the next week.

ALABAMA RECIPE BOX: CORNBREAD, 1862

Flour, for structure,
for bread so strong
it can stand the summer heat
without once asking for water.

Cornmeal, for grit
and that satisfying chew.

Slip in a little sugar
to make it all smile,
and baking powder
to puff it up
like a body in the heat.

Buttermilk—cool and thick
and just sour enough
to turn that bread savory.

Hot oil in the cast iron skillet
to make the crust crack.

Bake until golden.

Cut into squares,
for the little black ones
so they'll work an extra hour,
pick an extra row of cotton,
plow those fields til sundown.

LIST OF FAMOUS ALABAMA SLAVES

Jennie, who begat
Jake, who begat
Charity, Lizze, and Rev,
who begat
Esther, who begat
Daniel,
who begat
Dave, Georgia,
George, Emma,
Oliver, and Maugan,
who begat Alonza,
who bought his own farm,
which begat tomatoes
and carrots
and collard greens
and watermelons
and corn
and green beans
and blackberries
and a single perfect peach,
and absolutely
never
any
cotton.

INGREDIENT LIST: BLACK GIRL

big ass, big ass hair, natural and artificial flavors (oil sheen, blue magic hair grease, cocoa butter, shea butter, just plain butter, styling gel, bacon grease), all forms of supple (lips like pillows, finger-sink-able thighs, even the toes are voluptuous), murderous hips, intelligence (book learning, street learning, lyrics and poetry), a little extra joint in the neck (suitable for rolling).

Not from concentrate. Do not refrigerate.

THE BALLAD OF PEARL BAILEY

Your mama picked you
from the bottom of the sea.
When you hit the open air,
a wail of pecan pie
and applewood spewed out—
baby girl with a voice like oak.
I have strung you
around my neck—
you, center jewel among
lesser balls of glass.
The oyster remembers you best—
baby black as rock
stuffed like snuff
under its thick lip.
It coated you in song
each night—
thick, dark chords
from a deep, deep throat.

CORN SILK BARBIE

Every woman must have a shape,
and the glass Coke bottle
is just the right one—
we remember
the cool sweet truth
we poured down our teenaged throats
and the fizz that made us forget
Alabama, Tuscaloosa Street,
empty town and waves of heat.

Mama made us—
me, sister, and Birmingham cousins—
shuck corn on the back porch stairs.
Now, the green husks
are perfect cloth for an evening gown,
the silks for hair—
what man can resist that sweet, wet shine
of summer corn?

The mouth of the soda bottle
is as ripe as a scalp,
and our giggles
are just shrill enough
to match the glass clinks
our dolls make
as they dance at our command
and shimmy to our twinkling,
muddy, imagined beat.

GREGORY HINES COMES IN A VISION

I syncopate for you
on the kitchen tiles
in my rubber slippers.
I find you, thudding and electric
in the balls and pads of my barefeet—
your nonchalant hiccup
out of my unhinged wrists.

Shim sham angel,
pass your ghostly hands over me,
wiggle your buoyant ankles
and give me those rows
of tight-cornered teeth.

I will wait for you
in the half beat—
and-a there and-a then
you will carry me
on your metallic, clicking wings,
and we'll dig-spank
shuffle-hop
buffalo
into heaven's closing red curtain.

What about us said
we were on fire? What said
extinguish quickly,

fill up the hose and
set the dogs loose? Could they smell
our confusion? Or

was it our singing?
Were our voices like sirens,
a chorus of blood?

We were wet black seeds
in that raw Birmingham flesh—
we germinated.

Did the photos show
our fingers stretching like roots?
Did they show our eyes,

how they reached sunward,
to the hot, bright, silent star
that could turn water

to steam, seeds to fruit?
Did they see themselves become
our fertilizer?

SYMPHONY OF GOD—HYMN TO OUR JESUS

After the 1963 bombing of the 16th Street Baptist Church, Welsh artist John Petts created a stained glass window featuring a Black crucified Christ figure with his hands open and outstretched. The window was sent to the 16th Street Church in Birmingham, Alabama, and was installed and dedicated in 1965.

Oh, God. Let us be loyal
to your emerald-cut face,
give us your facets
in gulping doses, through veins
and the twiggy sparrow's song,
give us your mouth boiling with blood

on the Cross. Holy spittle, holy blood,
Lord, we will wash in you. Our loyal
bathing is a hymn, a baptismal song
for you. Jordan River, steamy Alabama, we face
you in our own watery faces. Palms up, veins
exposed, we are but faucets

awaiting you. We know you, multifaceted:
God of the medicinal blood,
God of the angry and the vain,
God who can pull you up from down low—cast all
your cares upon his glass-cut face
and you'll hear him before long. His song

is power—it is fertile, a womb-song.
There are faces in his facets,
crook-nose, flat-nose, and wide—face
it, children, nothing's certain but the blood,
he is porcelain *and* charcoal, loyal
to all who find him, all who witness his veins

bearing bread and wine. His veins
plucking bass behind a wailing song—
In the Evening, I'll be Loyal,
In the Evening, Precious Lord. In the facets
of a window, he waits for Sunday's blood.
He shakes himself loose into the faces

of worshippers, wills them to face
his Spirit, its trembling, its stinging in the veins,
its *Hallelujah, the Blood, the Blood!*
We will wash in white robes and sway a song
to him, wade our human feet into rivers, facets
of his gemstone grace. We wash, forever loyal.

Our eyes, the color of blood, the water's forceful song.
Under the tide, a face, a force. Our veins
spread and open, facets on our skin. Find us, forever loyal.

THE HISTORY BOOKS HAVE FORGOTTEN
HORACE KING

because history prefers its slaves
to stay shackled,
or, like Moses, take freedom
from God alone.
But, Sojourner Truth wore similar chains,
and Frederick Douglass knew the whip
like the back of his own chapped body,
and history tucked them neatly
under its thin white arms.

Perhaps, because he wasn't
all the way black—
he was poured half full of Creek,
filled with it from cheekbone to chest.

Maybe it was his profession,
because who really cares about a carpenter
unless he's Jesus?
But Horace *made* things:
bridges with panpipe walls,
bridges with crisscrossing arches,
Confederate warships to fight the good fight—
his brain was not too black for this;
wars are color blind,
especially when what you build
doesn't break.

He bought himself
from the state of Alabama
for fifteen hundred dollars
and a bridge.
He built a spiral spine of stairs
at the state capitol
and stretched his name,
wood and steel and cement,
over all its rivers
for the wanderer to walk over
and wonder who done it.

ON MARTIN LUTHER KING DAY, A NOOSE IS HUNG ON A TREE IN BLOUNT COUNTY

a golden shovel variation after Lucille Clifton

Tonight, a noose drips from a branch like corn syrup. If you listen,
you can hear it plunk and pool at the roots. You wonder
if this is Blount County, if this is 2014, if this city
is civilized, if you are a time machine of a woman,
travelled back to this dim geography,
when Alabama is pulpy, ready to pluck its own
stale fruit. You are thirsty, so you listen
for the sound of water—your tongue is a map
of desert, and suddenly there's just the noose and you,
darkness rolling out in all directions,
the stinging of so much quiet—a dust storm of silence. You
think, *maybe it's a joke. Nothing to fear—fear is what happens when
you listen to too much CNN.* The noose is still. It says, *you are a wom-
an, you are black, you are in the middle of Noplace, Alabama,
and if I catch you, I will wring you til you're anonymous,
til you're not even a black girl, you're just some damn body.*

VIRGIN MARY, RE-IMAGINED

as my paternal grandmother

head adorned in blue-gray curls,
nestled in the gold wool of her easy chair,
she cannot walk without help—
ankles swollen with our pain,
square, heavy glasses to magnify her God-stained eyes

as my cancer-stricken aunt

the light of her sickroom, a silvery blue,
her row of concave teeth shining in the shadow
of the IV pole, full cheeks prevailing despite
the tender sickness in her ovaries—   her
string of breathy jokes defy
the finite sound of her golden voice

as my maternal grandmother

her hands, stained and cracking from the washwater,
her shoulders sturdy—yoked for rearing,
she is a powerful shield for all her daughters,
ones birthed and ones found,
a psalm edges out of her small brown mouth,
grace, whole and white in her overflowing smile,
dotted with gold, precious teeth

as my blind aunt

the loud television in her blue-black bedroom,
the sweets, tucked like children, in her cheeks,
a cross of light gleams in her searching eyes,
she answers our prayers in playing cards:
savior spade, King, Queen, Jack of our Jesus

as a mirror

our wombs, clean and soft and blue
our eyes, the color of holy magic
we dream of the taste of our own merciful milk
it flows, whisper white, into God's open mouth

HAPPINESS

Auntie, do they serve collards
and bitter rutabagas
and sweet, sweet cornbread up there?
Is there pound cake and lemonade,
potato salad and fried chicken?

Are you young again,
pulled, finally,
from the dim trailer
and the buzz and break
of your police scanner?
Were you scared, Auntie,
or tired of the cesspools
and old roads of Greensboro, Alabama?

Auntie, are you still blind
in Heaven?
Can you finally watch
the colors change
on the TV made of clouds?

Will you grow long hair up there?
Will your dark skin still glow
and be called beautiful?

Is there insulin in Heaven?
Do you still use Sweet'n Low?
You'll probably have doughnuts for days,
and when we're all together again,
it'll be a big laughing party
full of glazed ham and candied yams
and good, thick blues.

GOSPEL OF THE GRITS

Nothing good in life comes without stirring—
the promise of butter, the salty whirring
of pressure in a pot. Breakfast comes naturally
in the South—wake up, bacon. Wipe eyes, biscuit dough.
Sting of coffee silenced by sugar, kiss of milk.
Grits, stones made soft with water and time,
when I think of you, I think of heat
and your chorus of fiery *amen*s when you reach a boil.
Some know you as fire,
I know you as love on a Sunday morning,
burning reassurance on the first day of school,
the perfect canvas for sausage gravy—
a soup of mornings and southern mothers,
goodness in bellies all over America,
hot spit of breakfast—peppery and white.

COMING OF AGE

I was baptized at eighteen—
the same year I had my first kiss.
I remember the pool and its cool, the sheen
of chapstick on my boyfriend's lips.
I remember that night in my driveway, the hiss
of my boyfriend's car as it cooled down.
I remember the preacher's hands, the fear I would drown

in all that water,
turn up dead, but at least I'd be clean,
washed by this version of my heavenly father.
Those blackboy lips had seemed
just as wet as the big holy pool—I leaned
away from that awful mouth, the tongue
that made me wash my face with soap—there's no fun

in french kissing. Or baptisms.
But I believed in both because I thought
my life was empty without them.
Turns out, my God and my mouth
were just fine without
those washings—there is a holiness in being dry,
keeping one's distance from the cry

and pull of pews and lips.
I'll make my body a desert if it means
I'll be untouched, quietly holy, un-eclipsed
by a man and his mouth, his body, the machine
of romance and religion, the saline
of saliva and an indoor pool.

Maybe I'm just not ready to unspool
myself, become the open wound
all people become eventually,
open for licks of pain and the swish of newfound
love. As for me, I'm happy (am I, really?)
with my books and crochet needles,
stacks of things that can't reject or respond
or suck me in like a baptismal pond.

SOJOURNER TRUTH SPEAKS TO HER DAUGHTER, 1843

My girl, you do not want to repeat my life.
I birthed you kids, standing up, right here by this stove.
I watched one die still dressed in my blood.

I saw them beat your father
because owned things can't love on a plantation.
I saw welts volcano and spurt out all over him.
I watched his love slide out like pus.

You do not want my tall, my strong,
you do not want the wrinkles on my face.
People say I strolled away from slavery
like it was a Sunday matinee.
I made speeches, I made words boom.
I can make a mean pan of biscuits. Thick gravy.
I can feed five children from a single cut of pork.

You do not want too many children
from a new husband shoved into you.
You do not want unlove.
You do not want to sop up the afterbirth
with your own mop and pail.

You want to know the secret to birthing on your feet?
Just squat real low, and when you feel it,
honey, let the tide flow.

RIDDLED IN THE HEART OF DIXIE

I am the tail of a kite in the Birmingham sky.

I am the crumb of hair between the teeth of an afro pick,
the slats of butter in biscuit dough.

I am Sheriff Taylor's clear breaths in that backcountry whistle,
the rocks beating beneath Opie's country toes.

I am the smell of fatback in a cast iron skillet,
the crust flaked off of cornbread in the oven.

I am the sparkling bellies of trains as they pass by Railroad Park.

I am the pothole cupping a tire,
the red dirt on the hill near grandmother's house,
I am the sour and the grain.

I am the lemonade and pound cake,
the gulp of air in *y'all*.

I am the tick of stars becoming brilliant in the sky.

Open your mouth and let me land on your tongue.

Let me wash you in Alabama heat
and tell you who you are.

ACKNOWLEDGEMENTS

Many thanks to the editors of the following publications, in which versions of following pieces appear or are forthcoming:

Academy of American Poets ("Viewing a KKK Uniform at the Civil Rights Institute")

DIME Magazine ("Birmingham Fire and Rescue")

Fjords Review Black American Edition ("nem")

Geoffrey Philp's *Literary Blog* ("Teaching J To Read")

Harvard Journal of African American Public Policy ("What the Glass Eye Saw," "The first time I heard about slavery," "Elegy," "Sojourner Truth Speaks to Her Daughter, 1843," and "slaves for sale")

Jai-Alai Magazine ("Virgin Mary Re-Imagined")

Kinfolks Quarterly ("The History Books Have Forgotten Horace King")

Lucid Moose Lit's Like a Girl: Perspectives on Feminine Identity Anthology ("spinster" and "What It Means To Say Sally Hemings")

Night Owl ("spin·ster" and "In The Beginning, There Was A Sound")

Pluck! ("Viewing a KKK Uniform at the Civil Rights Institute")

PMS poemmemoirstory ("De Soto Leaves a Negro," "Birmingham Fire and Rescue Haiku, 1963," "How To Make Your Daughters Culturally Aware and Racially Content During Christmastime," "List of Famous Alabama Slaves," "Corn Silk Barbie")

Prelude ("(I'm Blue) The Gong Gong Song, or, America the Beautiful," "Poem for Revolution")

Steel Toe Review ("Addie, Carole, Cynthia, Denise," "Rammer Jammer," "Salat Behind Al's Mediterranean and American Food")

Tough Times in America Anthology ("On Martin Luther King Day, A Noose Is Hung On A Tree In Blount County," "Sammy Davis, Jr. Sings to Mike Brown, Jr.," and "The men come for Emmett and Tamir and Michael and Eric and John and Trayvon and...")

Valley Voices New York School Special Edition ("Symphony of God—A Hymn to Our Jesus," "What It Means To Say Sally Hemings," "Gregory Hines comes in a Vision," and "The Ballad of Pearl Bailey")

NOTES

"On Martin Luther King Day, A Noose Is Hung In Blount County" and "The men come for Emmett and Tamir and Michael and Eric and John and Trayvon and…" are variations on the golden shovel form. Instead of including the entire inspiration piece in the new poem, I have included only the end words of each line in the inspiration poem. "The men come" began as a golden shovel, but through revision, became more of a golden almost-shovel. Some of Brooks's end words remain.

"On Martin Luther King Day a Noose is Hung In Blount County" is written using the end lines of "what the mirror said" by Lucille Clifton.

"The men come for Emmett and Tamir and Michael and Eric and John and Trayvon and…" is written using the end lines of "A Bronzeville Mother Loiters in Mississippi. Meanwhile, a Mississippi Mother Burns Bacon" by Gwendolyn Brooks.

Thank you Mom, Dad, Monique, Jasmine, and Julian for family and friendship. Denise, Campbell, Donna Aza for poetic guidance on this project. Many thanks to Derrick Austin for his poetic eye.

HUB CITY
PRESS

HUB CITY PRESS is a non-profit independent press in Spartanburg, SC that publishes well-crafted, high-quality works by new and established authors, with an emphasis on the Southern experience. We are committed to high-caliber novels, short stories, poetry, plays, memoir, and works emphasizing regional culture and history. We are particularly interested in books with a strong sense of place.

Hub City Press is an imprint of the non-profit Hub City Writers Project, founded in 1995 to foster a sense of community through the literary arts. Our metaphor of organization purposely looks backward to the nineteenth century when Spartanburg was known as the "hub city," a place where railroads converged and departed.

RECENT HUB CITY PRESS POETRY

Wedding Pulls • J.K. Daniels

Punch • Ray McManus

Pantry • Lilah Hegnauer

Voodoo For the Other Woman • Angela Kelly

Waking • Ron Rash

Home Is Where • Kwame Dawes, editor

Checking Out • Tim Peeler

Twenty • Kwame Dawes, editor